Learn SPANISH Through Fairy Tales

GOLDILOCKS and the 3 BEARS

Book Design & Production: Slangman Kids *(a division of Slangman Inc. and Slangman Publishing)*

Copy Editor: Julie Bobrick
Illustrated by: "Migs!" Sandoval
Translator: Marcela Redoles

Copyright © 2006 by David Burke

Published by: Slangman Kids *(a division of Slangman Inc. and Slangman Publishing)* 12206 Hillslope Street, Studio City, CA 91604 •USA • Toll Free Telephone from USA: 1-877-SLANGMAN (1-877-752-6462) • From outside the USA: 1-818-SLANGMAN (1-818-752-6462) • Worldwide Fax 1-413-647-1589 • Email: info@slangman.com • Website: www.slangman.com

"Migs!" Sandoval ✳ our illustrator ✳

Miguel *"Migs!"* Sandoval has been drawing cartoons since the age of 6 and has worked on numerous national commercials and movies as a sculptor, model builder, and illustrator. He was born in Los Angeles and was raised in a bilingual household, speaking English and Spanish. He currently lives in San Francisco where he is working on his new comic book series!

ISBN10: 1891888-803
ISBN13: 978189888-809
Printed in the U.S.A.

10 9 8 7 6 5 4 3 2 1

Order Form

Preview chapters & shop online!
www.slangman.com

SHIP TO: _____

_____

_____

_____

Contact/Phone/Email: _____

SHIPPING

Domestic Orders

SURFACE MAIL
(Delivery time 5-7 business days).
Add $5 shipping/handling for the first item, $1.50 for each
additional item.

RUSH SERVICE
Available at extra charge. Contact us for details.

International Orders

SURFACE MAIL
(Delivery time 6-8 weeks).
Add $6 shipping/handling for the first item, $2 for each
additional item. Note that shipping to some countries may be
more expensive. Contact us for details.

AIRMAIL (approx. 3-5 business days)
Available at extra charge. Contact us for details.

Method of Payment (Check one):

☐ Personal Check or Money Order
  (Must be in U.S. funds and drawn on a U.S. bank.)

☐ VISA ☐ Master Card ☐ Discover ☐ American Express ☐ JCB

Credit Card Number
☐☐☐☐☐☐☐☐☐☐☐☐☐☐☐☐☐☐☐

_____ ☐☐☐☐
Signature   Expiration Date

QTY	ISBN-13	TITLE	PRICE	LEVEL	TOTAL COST
	English to CHINESE (Mandarin)				
	9781891888-793	Cinderella	$14.95	1	
	9781891888-854	Goldilocks	$14.95	2	
	9781891888-915	Beauty and the Beast	$14.95	3	
	English to FRENCH				
	9781891888-755	Cinderella	$14.95	1	
	9781891888-816	Goldilocks	$14.95	2	
	9781891888-878	Beauty and the Beast	$14.95	3	
	English to GERMAN				
	9781891888-762	Cinderella	$14.95	1	
	9781891888-830	Goldilocks	$14.95	2	
	9781891888-885	Beauty and the Beast	$14.95	3	
	English to HEBREW				
	9781891888-922	Cinderella	$14.95	1	
	9781891888-939	Goldilocks	$14.95	2	
	9781891888-946	Beauty and the Beast	$14.95	3	
	English to ITALIAN				
	9781891888-779	Cinderella	$14.95	1	
	9781891888-823	Goldilocks	$14.95	2	
	9781891888-892	Beauty and the Beast	$14.95	3	
	English to JAPANESE				
	9781891888-786	Cinderella	$14.95	1	
	9781891888-847	Goldilocks	$14.95	2	
	9781891888-908	Beauty and the Beast	$14.95	3	
	English to SPANISH				
	9781891888-748	Cinderella	$14.95	1	
	9781891888-809	Goldilocks	$14.95	2	
	9781891888-861	Beauty and the Beast	$14.95	3	
	Japanese to ENGLISH 絵本で えいご を学ぼう				
	9781891888-038	Cinderella	$14.95	1	
	9781891888-045	Goldilocks	$14.95	2	
	9781891888-052	Beauty and the Beast	$14.95	3	
	Korean to ENGLISH 동화를 통한 ENGLISH 배우기				
	9781891888-076	Cinderella	$14.95	1	
	9781891888-106	Goldilocks	$14.95	2	
	9781891888-113	Beauty and the Beast	$14.95	3	
	Spanish to ENGLISH Aprende INGLÉS con cuentos de hadas				
	9781891888-953	Cinderella	$14.95	1	
	9781891888-960	Goldilocks	$14.95	2	
	9781891888-977	Beauty and the Beast	$14.95	3	

Total for Merchandise ☐
Sales Tax *(California residents only add applicable sales tax)* ☐
Shipping *(See left)* ☐
ORDER GRAND TOTAL ☐

Prices subject to change

(a division of Slangman Publishing)

** TO PLACE AN ORDER - CALL, FAX, OR EMAIL: **
Phone: 1-818-752-6462 • Fax: 1-413-647-1589
Email: info@slangman.com • Web: www.slangman.com
12206 Hillslope Street • Studio City, CA 91604

(FORM 071606)

Dedication

The entire "Foreign Language Through Fairy Tales" series is dedicated to all the children of the world.

It is through their understanding, appreciation, and celebration of our differences that the world will become a better and safer place for us all.

One thing to remember...

The words in *green italics* throughout this fairy tale are words you've already learned in the previous level! Do you still remember what they mean?

1

oso →

papá →

mamá →

Once upon a time, there was a [bear] family who lived in a *casa* in the forest — a [papa] **oso**, a [mama] who was very *bonita*, and their pride and joy, the cutest

2

baby oso. The **bebé oso** was very little.

The **pequeño bebé oso** was also very

guapo like his **papá**. The **papá oso** was very

much *enamorado* with the **mamá** and they

bebé

pequeño

3

were both very proud of their family. One day, the **mamá** prepared some soup for lunch, but it was too hot. While it cooled off,

paseo ← the **oso** family decided to go for a stroll .

Meanwhile in a town nearby, there lived a **muchacha** named Goldilocks who was very **bonita**, but also very **triste** because she never had anything fun to do.

5

She thought for a **momento** and came up with an idea. She decided to take a **paseo** in the forest. Very soon, she came upon a *casa* and knocked on the door but no one

puerta

6

cansada

was there. So she opened the **puerta**, put one *pie* inside the *casa*, and said "Hello? Is anyone home?" She was very ⟨tired⟩ after her long **paseo** and since no one answered,

7

mesa ←

cocina ←

she walked inside the *casa*. She looked around for a *momento* and was very *felíz* to see a [table] in the [kitchen] with food piled high on it!

Goldilocks quickly walked toward the **mesa** in the **cocina** and was super extra *felíz* because there on the **mesa** in the **cocina** was a [bowl] –

→ **tazón**

9

uno
dos
tres

but not just (one), not just (two), but (three)! **Uno**, **dos**, **tres**! And the smell from each **tazón** was wonderful! So, she took a taste from the first **tazón** that belonged to

the **papá oso** and said, "This is too hot !"
Then she took a taste from the **tazón** that
belonged to the **mamá** and said, "Oh! This
is too cold !" Then she took a taste from

caliente

frío

the **tazón** of the **pequeño bebé oso** and said, "Ahhh. This one isn't too **caliente**. It isn't too **frío**. It's just right!" And she ate everything in the **tazón**. "*Gracias!*" she said to the

empty **tazón**. Well, now she was even more **cansada** than ever after eating so much food. So, she decided to rest. In the living room, she saw a [chair]...but not just

silla

uno, not just **dos**, but **tres**! **Uno**, **dos**, **tres**! So, she sat down in the **silla** of the **papá oso**, which was very *grande*, and said, "Oh! This **silla** is definitely too

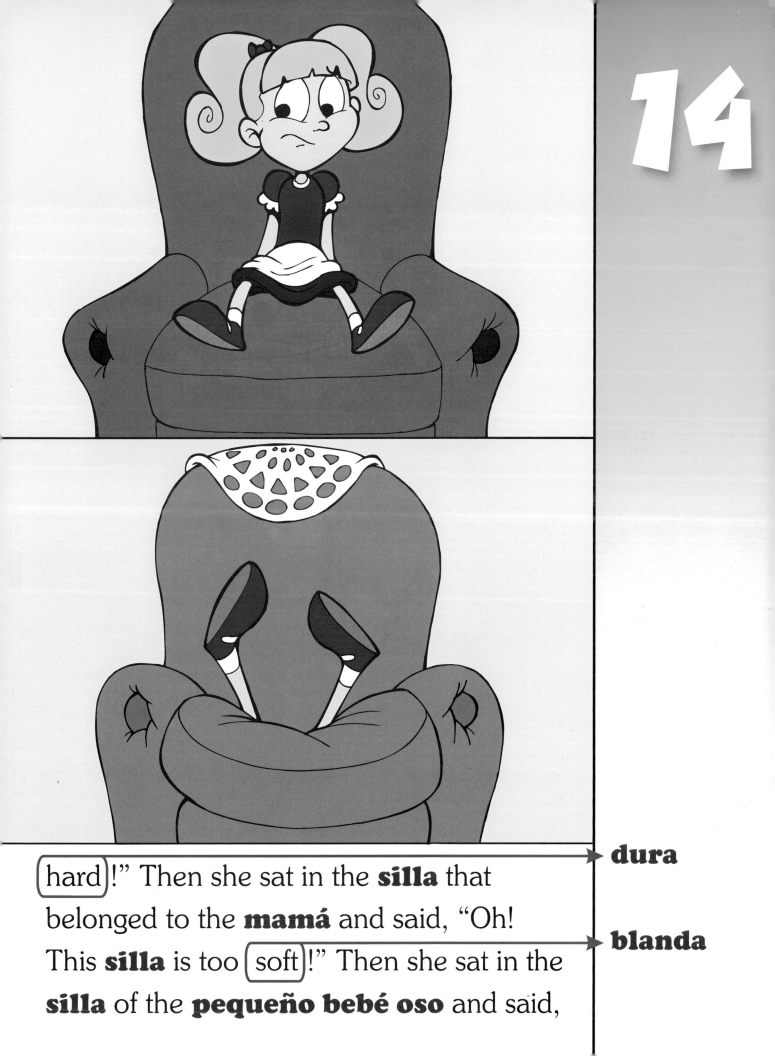

hard)!" Then she sat in the **silla** that
belonged to the **mamá** and said, "Oh!
This **silla** is too (soft)!" Then she sat in the
silla of the **pequeño bebé oso** and said,

→ **dura**

→ **blanda**

"Ahhh. This **silla** isn't too **dura**. It isn't too **blanda**. It's just right!" But just as she got comfortable… *Crack!* The **silla** of the **pequeño bebé oso** completely fell apart!

Still **cansada**, she decided to look for the bedroom to take a little nap. In front of her, she saw a bed ...but not just **uno**, not just **dos**, but **tres**! Uno, dos, tres!

→ **cama**

So, she tried the **cama** of the **papá oso** and said, "This **cama** is too **dura**!" Then she tried the **cama** that belonged to the **mamá** and said, "This **cama** is too **blanda**!"

Then she tried the **cama** of the **pequeño bebé oso** and said, "Ahhh. This **cama** isn't too **dura**. It isn't too **blanda**. It's just right!" And she fell fast asleep.

At that very **momento**, the **oso** family returned from their **paseo**. But upon entering the *casa*, the **papá oso** noticed something. "Someone's been eating my soup!" he said.

"And someone's been eating my soup!"
said the **mamá** who was very confused.
"And someone's been eating MY soup and
ate it all up!" cried the **pequeño bebé oso**.

21

The **papá oso** walked into the living room and was very surprised at what he saw. "Look!" he said angrily. "Someone's been sitting in my **silla**!"

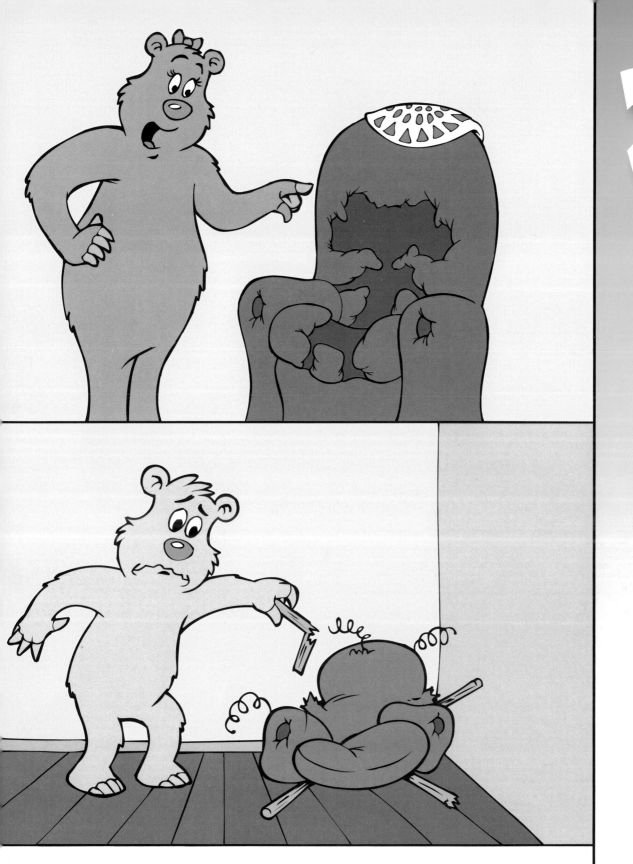

"And someone's been sitting in my **silla**!" said the **mamá**. "And someone's been sitting in MY **silla** and broke it into pieces!" cried the poor **pequeño bebé oso**.

Then the **oso** family heard snoring coming from the bedroom, so they went in to look. Something wasn't right. "Someone's been sleeping in my **cama**!" said the **papá oso**.

"And someone's been sleeping in my **cama**" said the surprised **mamá**. "And someone's been sleeping in MY **cama** and there she is!" shouted the **pequeño bebé oso**.

At that very **momento**, Goldilocks woke up and saw the entire **oso** family! The **oso** family thought the young *muchacha* was very *mala* to use their *casa* without

permission! "Oh, *gracias!*" she said to the **papá oso**. "*Gracias* for letting me eat food from your **tazón**, sit in your **silla**, and lie in your **cama**! *Gracias!*"

she said again, expecting the **oso** family to say, "*De nada!*" But they were angry that she caused so much trouble in their *casa* and the **oso** family growled at her.

So, she slowly stood up on the **cama** of the
pequeño bebé oso, and said nervously,
"Well, *gracias* for having me and...
Adiós!" And with that, Goldilocks jumped

off the **cama**, and dashed out the front **puerta**, running as fast as each *pie* could move. Needless to say, she never returned to visit the *casa* of the **oso** family again!